JUVENILE JUSTICE SYSTEM DETERMINING AGE OF JUVENILE: INDIA

BY ASHISH TIWARI EDITED BY ISHITA CHATTERJEE

The Book is dedicated to Scholars and Academecians

Contents

CHAPTER ONE

Juvenile Justice determing age of juvenile

1.1 Introduction

Juvenile legal system in India consist of crime committed by children in conflict of law there various age from under 18 under 16 and rest there are various principal associated with it and an act which was passed by central government in 2015 juvenile justice act which consist of all rule and procedure followed in providing punishment in rehabilitation and adoption of child proper care and rule and procedure followed by authority dealing with child as child at age do act to look cool do not have full understanding of right and wrong and crime committed by them and punishment provided there life could have a serious impact and could damage there whole life so proper method with rule and procedure are followed.

There been recent many debate and public outrage on child issues and trying them as adults and while following various un policy and guidelines it all been decided by government. As children are future of this country and more population of our country are below 18 in the advancement in technology and availability of internet we all have responsibility to make youth in spending more time in learning and gaining knowledge not get caught in drugs and child employment. Constitution of India protect rights of children in various article 15 article 39 article 45 article 47 which ensures states to protect right and care, education for children. These all along with un rules and policy all help in protecting children in conflict of law.

Public awareness knowing legal rights and are most important and help in making a better society for all. With increase in number of cases in crime by children are rapid increasing and to new methods need to be adopted by central government of India to end stop these crime rate. State too with its jurisdiction frame new laws which help in protecting rights of child and promote rights and duties and provide care environment where child can easily grow learn and become good citizens follow rule and regulation and become law abiding citizens of our country. Youth can lead with great examples and become a leader and guide our citizens.

Various laws which are adopted by different country which follow our legal system can be taken as reference and adopted and implemented by government here country such as America uk Canada developed nations and developing nations their rule can be followed and implemented. Supreme courts and high courts should also help in setting up good precedence and various ngo and other welfare organizations should also help in awareness and ministry to work in implementing new rules and policy empowers knowledge and guide children's in schools. Books like ncert and other boards should help in guiding children's and

help them in learning new methods and with examples movies too need to be made animated and help teach people with moral values and with rights and duties.

1.2 History [1]

The juvenile justice system in india is based on the principal of protecting children in 1986 jja act juvenile justice act was made by parliament decided to replace the children act in various state in india this act contains all un standards of rule of administration of juvenile justice rules of 1985 it mas made and help to care protect treatment and development of childrens than also hope and promised did not covers all expectations of citizens and not proper implementation in 1992 un convention on the rights of child rules made and india ratified it for need of more child friendly rules made which all lead to a jja act 2000 was passed juvenile justice care and protection of children act which replaced previous act of 1986.

Juvenile justice act 2000 was based on the principal of un convention protection of liberty

And clearly defining the age as of 18 year the act also based on the articles of constitution.

In 2006 many amendments were made to the 2000 jja act which includes child friendly approach, best interest of children proper care and constitution human rights crc un juvenile rule all included.

It help in clear all doubts that it shall apply to all cases of detention or criminal prosecution of juvenile under any other law, relevant date in determining the juvenility of a person and applicability of jja act

It also help in widen scope of adoption of a child to childless parents and limit to only citizens of India. With making support from central and state government making regulations and new rules with fulfilling changes need in society.

Adoption foster care sponsorship after care organizations under rehabilitation and social reintegration alternatives. With state government rules and agency working with helping children's and various nonprofit organizations.

Cara guidelines and noc than all rule followed and help in adoption of child. Legal system lawyers and legal expert's health system doctor's forensic expert all required to work in together and help children.

Teachers and ngo work together in hand to help children's and many methods adopted in teaching learning and helping children to overcome fears and become good citizens of our country.

Media both digital and print media help in creating awareness and reporting child exploitation and bring attention to the society and concerned authority and help children's here by following guidelines and protecting identity of child and help them in big ways.

We as a citizen need to be aware about rights and duty while fulfilling all duties we as a society have moral duty to look after another human being and help them in any ways by donation by teaching we can help them overcome and become citizens ready for future.

Development of Juvenile Justice System in India

In the past 70 years of independence a better ways are made for children and improved in our country. Constitution uphold and protects various Fundamental Rights

Fundamental Duties and Directive Principles of State Policy which protects

care of survival, needs, development and protection of children in our country.

1.3 MEANING

juvenile meaning defined question what is juvenile?

With following all acts and with accordance to latest act 2015 with specific mention of under section 2 of the act it states as a children whose age is bellow 18 year which further defines as children who have not attained a adult hood who are teenager not to be treated as adult with according to law of the nations and cannot be tried or held legally accountable for his/her criminal act.

The juvenile in conflict of law with law of the nation. Juvenile term used in various legal terms in notifying a teenage criminal offender and minor meaning not in legal capacity to be consent consideration to legal without presence of guardians and parents.

1.4 JUVENILE DELIQUENCY

Question arises next what is juvenile delinquency?

Delinquency is the difference in attitude behavious of the children or different abnormal behaviour of the child. Delinquent main reference to a child different behaviour to other people shows illegal disturbed behaviour and have taken a different ways mainly illegal ways to live a normal social life accepted the fake cool life to be adjusted in society. But in real sense these behaviour is harmfull to the society and we in legal terms defines as juvenial delinquent there age is the most important and both for boy or girls under age 18 years.

These are list below of acts and behaviour which are not good for children-

1 staying out late in night and living at different places running from home without informing the parents and guardians.

2 misbehaviours with all age of people and repeating habitually.

3 abusing friends and family verbally in friends group.

4 starting gambling betting at young age

5 commiting sexual offences bad touch

6 looting super stores mobile phones chain snaching

7 started stealing mobiles and selling for cash

Juvenile children's tend to commit criminal offences through self or in now group of organisation there are few factors which can make them hard-core criminal listed below

First

school not attending and bunking and missing classes in between first of the reason of not satisfied with the school life due to missing off sports art good teachers which can teach them new skills or New good habits some ways teacher lack in motivating student due to large number of student presence in class the ratio between student and teacher is more than not sufficient and lack of good example end teaching method with changing in Technology these things disappoint children and does not motivate them in attending school the regular absentees or not going to schools attending class start their wasting time in smoking Drug abuse gambling Eve teasing and do theft.

second

Entertainment industry through films TV and online pornographic content these obscene content are easily available in mobile phone and on computers which are easily accessible to all children these content provoke sexually and other ways In teenager which later on due to hormonal changes as growing up these desire to look cool The teenagers commit crime As in an new adventure to experience

Desire adventuring new experience in pressure from friend circle juvenile gets excited from Reading sexExperience of adults and other hard-core criminal

Weather after into the view of doctors and analyzing the Psychiatrist they clearly define Deliquency is actually build up of upon principal of pleasure and pain they want to gain maximum satisfaction to overcome their needs and do their good work or bad work therefore they became victim to their own bad behaviour and there are environmental factors also which result in Deliquency

we need to accept this that deliquency cannot be just solved by making rules and regulation but it need a global effort of the society in our country there are many acts such as child act from 1960 and JJa act which helps in covering all the needs and demand of children and protecting and caring them we need to build up a society so that each child should be given proper attention care and knowledge so that is not May feel alone or left out in a crowd We as a parent and guardian should also look out the needs of the children with the global Efort need to be put off so that safer place could be build for all of us.

1.5 Legislative reforms development

In our country the legislative development over than 70 years and in before independence the first regulation on juvenile was presented in 1850 the apprentice act which talks about proper schooling of children's In community and also providing relief and Care do the kids and rehabilitation methods were adopted for the kids who are accused or convicted through the "Process of trial of court between the age group of 10 to 18 years this act was present and was used for 30 years then in 1897 reforms were done on school which is popularly known as reform school act which was used for century and then major improvement for schools and teaching method for all children's are adopted for all community and literacy rate was improved after that we have child act 1960 page in later chapters we will discuss about We have juvenile Justice 1986 which primally changes the whole definition of juvenile and created a better system for juvenile Justice from preventing children from conflict of law new methods act and regulation were adopted and provided safety and good environment for children to preserve their childhood with accepting the rule and regulation of United nation This 1986 act changed and framed a uniform law to be adopted throughout the country beside in the State Jammu and Kashmir before the passing of this act each state have different set of regulation for the children after the passage of facts from Parliament the uniforms code was adopted and accepted by all state

From the year 1990 this juvenile issue got heated up and attention from all people and [1]society establish heated debate were conducted on this topic to frame policy regionally and in our acepted by whole country which result in influencing the Ministry of social Justice agreed an authorised and drafting new for policy regarding juvenile justice system in our country and came forward with juvenile Justice act 2000 the Indian government with the enactment and enforcement of this act abolished the previous act of juvenile Justice 1986 it was again amended in the year 2006 so that it cope up with the new requirement of the Junveniel policy throughout the country and accepted our state making it with keeping in mind the United Nations policy and Child rights acepted globally the main objective of the act was to change the law concerning offenders and juvenile with proper attention given to specific areas such as protection care by the authority during the trial and after the trial all required attention were given to the child and these approaches were adopted certain goals were taken into consideration while framing these policies and adopting this mechanism in the year 2007 the government of India came forward with NCPCR which is popularly known as national committee for the protection of Child rights in my march 2007

main objective of this committee was that to ensure to ensure to all the rules and regulation policies drafted with respect to the children which were accepted by the state should be implemented properly and in a peaceful manner the regional district was marked to promote the policy in the district and these areas were marked by the authority awareness campaign was also started so that the lot of children parents and guardians can get educated and accept how to be safe and treat child within the society different selected groups were made which are known as committee whose main work was to proper implementation of rules and policy of the government and awareness within the society and help them to learn and mingle within the society and are aware with their rights and duty towards your nation

seventh United nation Congress was organised and agreed to prepare a very beautiful model for the children so that lives of children can be improved and get better with the global standard with following the rights and duty Constitution of India also provides in their article specifically in article 15 with child rights and these methods were adopted by the all juvenile Justice board in their districts and in the states which require that all three model first the due process security second third in to make awareness and believe in the juvenile justice system and believe in justice for

all These three models covers the economic and social impact of study of children with and conflict of law so that prevention can be taken to put the end to rise in crime records and improve our rules and regulation throughout the changing needs of the society with a proper rehabilitation method also so that after conviction And punishment the juvenile is taken back to the society where they are a justice given and accepted by all and they further

do not commit any crime or do not fall in any organisation whose main purpose was to exploit these young children into criminal world criminal world.

CHAPTER TWO

INDIAN AND INTERNATIONAL LEGAL FRAMEWORK ALL ACTS RULES AND PROCEDURE

2.1 The Children Act 1960

In our country , there was a great rise of the number of

neglected and delinquent child in nutrition education and forceful child labor. New policy and rule and regulation programs took up in methods of five year plan to meets the needs of neglected child. New era of Industrialization coupled with urbanization also brought different type of problems for child.

questions and conflicts was present as in number of rise in reporting and cases of juvenile delinquency in all over country and in number of cases most popular offence was theft because of less rules and regulation laws that governs with delinquent juveniles present in small number of states therefore the present government of that time made and passed the Children Act 1960. First drawback was the Act, was enforced and applied to the union territory of India but it was a founding step which help states to follow and make their own Children Acts.

The child act help in providing care support welfare new education policy helping in improving life of left out and not taken proper care of children through this policy first time in our country detention of child juvenile is prohibited in any circumstances it has made a separate legal authority to help in dealing with juvenile and made new children courts and the boards through this act three tire institution of legal system was introduced first consist of supervision home for juvenile whose day throughout the proceeding second method was providing home for these juvenile children's and third system consist of providing education through special homes and schools and also for sex discriminatory definition mention of child with respect to age for boy it was below 16 year and for girls it was below 18 years of age all the states excepted these rules and regulation but age Differ from state to state so there was different treatment in different areas throughout the country

2.2 Juvenile Justice Act 1986

. As the many state adopted and Made rules on children's in conflict of law so there was a need in a society to adopt a uniform rules and regulation any laws regarding juvenile there for in 1986 juvenile Justice act was made to keep best interest of juvenile with changing in rapid demand of uniform rules through society while keeping in mind constitution rules an article and national policy resolution made in the year 1974 with adopting UN declaration of children rights and UN declaration on minimum standard method off administration governing juvenile properly known as Beijing rules made in 1985 the first rule and Justice act was made regarding detention which abolish the rule out detention and police lock up or jail

and made two specific authority first of a board which is known as juvenile Justice board " and a new ""juvenile court to Helping dealing with juvenile through this trials and various policy various recommendation and acceptance on these recommendation various institution were made for protection and providing security two juvenile through juvenile homes for proper treatment of Juvenile the special homes and supervision homes were made for juveniles which help them throughout the trial and after care to take care of juvenile these homes have proper supervision by authority and special treatment were given so that main motive was to protect these Juveniles from criminalization penalizing and for their Mental stigma.

With the Implementation of the new act the benefit of protecting rights and interest were made helping formation of new method towards securing justice within small period of time a lot of drawbacks and faults of the new act came forward and in the field of determining the age of the juvenile in the process of trial during the court trials with the proceeding Communicating the charges and to the parents guardians making report by the officers in rehabilitation and also in taking care of Juvenile who lives in this institution provided by authority don't really know the purpose of why they are living there and there was conflict in laws made by state with the new act In implementation as it

Violate The basic structure of the new act and also violation of authority boards protection homes "juvenile court and after-care house there were no proper or benchmark set by authority followed in adoption foster care education and in food these all drawbacks between the act and its implementation came forward when the new convention was made by United nation in the protection of children right in 1989 The government came aware of these rules made by United nation and recognize them in the year 1992 with the policy and rules of CRC to protect children from involvement conflict of law.

With the new CRC guidelinesOn the children in conflict of law were highly valued by the United nation in first Riyadh rules and second Rules on protection of Juvenile deprived of liberty both these rules and guidelines promoted and gave information about the process which need to be adopted globally for the juvenile of 18 years of age by 1993 a world conference was conducted on human rightsIn Vienna and with the adoption of Vienna declaration it was requested and specifically told to state to ratify and implement the CERC rules in India also authority and the government accepted these rules.

2.3 Juvenile Justice (Care & Protection of Children) Act 2000

By the time in 2000 year learning from the past and with development Government modifies the juvenile act to make it with the acceptance of CRC guidelines New act passed in the year 2000 which is named as juvenile Justice act 2000 it protect and promote justice and rights of children's and help mainly in protecting Child rights with a better name properly known as juvenile in conflict with law The Maine objective is to restrain the influence on

child who are in need of care and protection from those Who are involved in conflict of law it contain definition of child juvenile and it is accepted throughout the country except in the state Jammu and Kashmir the definition state and define is a person who has not completed 18 years of age and Java island conflict of law consist of all children's who are found to be committed an offence while dealing with its acts it also gives guidance parents guardians to how to protect and prevent their child from Delinquency and promote counselling to them it also provide broad choice Of community programs as an option to the juvenile.

The JJ Act 2000, made and passed with good policy and rules but it also have drawback with the insertion of certain substantive and procedural process. (Safe)

Age was clearly defined upto 18 yr age while determining the age of the juvenile many took this as better ways but as the act an acted and applied by year 2001 the whole of the region of country and accepted by all states in enforcing.

2.4 Juvenile Justice (Care and Protection of Children) (Amendment) Act 2006

By the year 2006 amendments was made which is specifically talk about Juvenility would be considered from the date of commission of offence which include the age group of people who have not completed 18 years and further clarified by a court in the case Arnit Das vs the state of Bihar these amendments made it clear in any circumstances or condition juvenile in conflict of law should be not kept in lock up or jail or in any custody and it further mention that CJM have every right to do review of the pendency of cases in the board within the time of 6 month and child protection units to be set up in every district And state to check up the proper implementation of the policy the act.(Safe)

2.5 Juvenile Justice Act 2015 (amedments)

The Juvenile Justice (Care and Protection of Children) Bill, 2015 was approved and passed

by Lok Sabha on 7th May, 2015 by majority ; and was passed by Rajya Sabha on

22nd December, 2015 with majority and received Presidential assent and came into force on 31st December 2015, to whole India except in the J&k state.

.

It provides section including provision for both the children first who are in need of care and who are in conflict with law when you definition were included for example abandoned orphaned surrendered children serious and heinous crimes committed by juveniles in further chapters power duty and function off juvenile Justice board were provided and Child welfare committee duty or pension which specify time limit in any case enquiry made by board and in further chapters section specifically talks about serious offences committed by juvenile above the age of 16 year and New adoption chapter it's been added which deal

with adoption of Orphaned and abandoned children and mandatory registration of these institution of child care.

2.6 National Human Rights Commission and Juvenile Justice System

National human right commission it's an independent Body to kept watch on protection of human rights in our country from the time being this commission has been made it raises concerns of all children who are in need of care protection throughout the country the commission is made to monitor the complaint against children, program new projects and policy and rule making at the national it also research on effective application of [1]international rules and regulation for help In functioning of juvenile justice system in our country. (Safe)

INTERNATIONAL CONVENTION ON CHILDS RIGHTS

2.7 UN Convention on the Rights of the Children

At the sixth United nation Congress on the new development on prevention of crime and treatment of offenders organized and Venezuela in 1980 where discussion was held in detail about setting up minimum standard rules for the administration of juvenile justice system and treat each child hazards human rights from the day he or she is born and it cannot be denied by anyone therefore there must be proper law to protect these rights of children and special attention need to be provided to homeles And street children in the urban city is to prevent juvenile Deliquency.

A child is defined by the UN on the rights of child CRC and age is defined as under 18 year it specifically mention childhood middle childhood and a Adolescent The convention on rights of children 1989 includes specific rights such as political several social cultural economic rights right to survival included the right to life good standard of living health also include nationality and identity right to protection include protection against exploitation inhuman treatment violence abuses sexual abuses and specific protection in critical problem In emergency armed conflict and in civil.

There are development and rights this included Education rights childhood care and overall development security cultural activities and re-creation right to expression it includes from the light of the child's freedom of speech and expression freedom of thoughts.

These convention help in providing legal remedy the children's and help them in providing security in the society The article 34 talks about duty of the states to protect the right of child from all type of sexual exploitation for enforcement of this article states are given power to take all necessary stepsA measure to prevent sexual activity unlawful to stop child prostitution Promise of a user children

Article 35 empowers state to take all appropriate national multilateral measures please stop and prevent abduction traffic in children sale of children in any way.

Article 36 empowers state to protect children from a new form of exploitation which prejudice any aspect of child welfare children need care and support to survive because the nature does not help protectChildren infant they need this protection by state till the age of adult Various policies and programmes are made to improve education skills health and nutrition home shelters for the development of children.

[1]CHAPTER 3 CONSTITUTIONAL PROVISION AS PROVIDED

Constitution provision

after the independence in the past 70 years many Constitution articles are present Which provide safety And care education nutrition of children with specific emphasis on protecting fundamental rights and directed states of policy briefly list of articles given below

article 15 sub clause 3 talk about state responsibility for women in general children in making special provision

article 21A talk about right to education it is the duty of the state to provide free and compulsory education to all children in the age group of 6 to 14 years

article 23 talk about traffic in human being and bonded labour it was a bit prohibit any form of bonded forced labour beggar and trafficking of any human being promote in the right of protecting the rights of children's

article 24 talks about working of children in factories hazardous mills Prohibit any children below the age of 14 from working in industries

article 30 E under dpsp provide health and strength of the children should not be abused and

F talk about providing ample labour protect opportunity to children to enjoy their childhood and not get exploited under any condition

CHAPTER 5 PREVENTION METHODS WITH AMENDMENTS

1Prevention of delinquency

First prevention is the effort was a society and the family friends in keeping children safe in the environment near home stop children from involving in any illegal activities and doing any sexual offences while growing up education is must so that they gain knowledge and become a better citizen and help each other in the need of the hour through education seminars conducting webinar we can motivate them help them solving problem and also communicate with them which is most important the people from the legal aid should also help and also people from non-government organisation Come forward and helping motivating JUVENILEs and discussing about rights and duties required to be followed and accepted by all and serving justice today rich or poor both childrens.

5.2 special police

Special needs to be given training need to be want provided to the police with explaining them the rights and duties which need to be followed while dealing with the general JUVENILE cases with the hierarchy of rank from constable to dcp the police should help while receiving complaints and proper action need to be done and a follow-up is done in the trial court. civil uniform should be used by the police so that the children do not get harassed or have fear of telling his/her story in front of police women or men police. police need to do counselling and guiding the JUVENILE throughout the trial process should accept this observation home and also keep informing informant so that they can get information which helps in prevention of crime and also build trust in our society enquiry done by the police should be completed within Time frame and recruitment of police should be done so that we have large number of police but people which provide safety and security and help in spreading own peace and harmony in society.

6 DETERMINING AGE OF THE JUVENILE

[1]Determination of age of juveniles

it is the responsibility power given to the court to decide and make a decision on age of the accused involved in crime act as the child in young age cannot be kept in prison with adult criminal or in jail special power are given in jja act to board authorities in making case and provide punishment on the basis of the documents such as school certificate municipal certificate and certified copy or through medical test it all records are submitted and then age is decided.

In the 1986 at the age of the juvenile is accepted as 16 year for both boys and girls but later on there were some changes in the age by the year 2000 the age was fixed by the government as 18 year for both boys and girls proper definition were given in the recent act 2015 the juvenile was defined

And heinous crime the juvenile to be treated as adult above 16 yr age and age to be decide on the date of crime and record mentioned and accepted in court with scrutiny done with certified copy original through this court decide whether the child is juvenile age or not if not found under age than to be treated as adult and many cases fake certificate are made by school authorities which later on proved wrong and age is not accepted by court proper inspection inquiry are conducted and done regarding scrutinising the age as its lawyers need to prove it verified with original than accepted otherwise medical test various are present with rapid improvement in technology which give results on by conducting test with the help of medical doctors experts

Jja 2015 has solved much extend this problem and with other provision also provide support and safety to children teenage as by through Indian penal code crpc criminal procedure code and main principle of doliincapax which help chidren of age group of 7 to 11 as they are not mature enough to be giving consideration and consent.

The court accepts after scrutiny of documents presented by the school records which were submitted during time of admission with passing the matric exams others documents are also considered as municipal authority which are given on birth death by records and also in some cases the medical examination are done on medical test such as bone test and x-rays and ossification test teeth present.

In the case **Emperor versus Mohammed** here the court ordered that the act committed by that children of throwing stones towards the train their children are being protected under the IPC 80 to 183 of Indian penal code as they wereFive and eight years of age

In case **Ashwini Kumar Saxena versus state of Madhya Pradesh** here the accused was charged with 302 of the IPC with 27 of arms act and with 34 of IPC the offence committed was on the day 19 October 2008 at 12:30 near the area of Chhatarpur which resulted in death of Yadav before the session Court they accused filed a petition in CJM court regarding the age of proving to be a juvenile and bail plea was also presented before the court CJM court CJM court order the bone test and very various other medical test with ex ray result of as a result of rest elbow leg knee and teeth with the opinion of the doctor it was clear that he was 20 years of age from the date of committing offence and the teeth x-ray teeth teeth came to be 32 teeth which resulted in making age more than 21 years has The court order that he's not juvenile at the time of offence.

In the case **Om Prakash versus State of Rajasthan** here the accused was tried of the committing offences under 376 of IPC and they have stand and plead guilty in the case one ground was availed whether by learn it counsel which claim that the accused is juvenile as per the definition of the juvenile Justice act 2000 the court trial ordered the juvenile test that at the date of the incident Was he the juvenile and the result came in school mark admission records and other medical test which prove that he was under her age of 18 And was treated for the rest as juvenile.

In the case **Umesh Chandra versus State of Rajasthan** A complete bench of apex court was sitting on the question of date of commission of offence at the fixed date for convening date of child act the view that was accepted as act apply on from the date and crime committed from that date the children JUVENILE mens rea need to be questioned to find motive crime act and crime reason if need to be treated as adult the question of enforcement of record and rule act passed was also examined and view were accepted as follows the act enforced through out our country.

In the case **arnit Das versus State of Bihar** a bench of apex court held that the first date of record of crime and the date of applicable of the act making the similar with the study of data criminal record throughout the year and region of state Section 32 of the act was detail [1]explain in this case which covers the age of the juvenile this resulted in maximum criticism from the society.

In **Maldah versus State of Gujarat** here the Gujarat High "Court Analyse the JJ act of 1986 with and obtaining the literal meaning of the word attained and further elaborated that the age of the boy to be considered as a JUVENILE should not be also be less than 16 and a girl should be no longer more than 18 as per the juvenile act of 1986.

Similarly in the case **Lal Mohammad was the state** the court observed that the faculty document on state of representative leads to the greater loss of the evidentiary value and as per the record of following Indian evidence act the other records or observed and the main focus was done on the medical board which conducted the test of the Petitioner and gave the results so here the medical importance were given more priority then other documents on determining age of the juvenile.

In the case **Rattan Lal versus state of Rajasthan** there was aid provided by the High Court under the supervision of authority first there were no enquiry made by the authority in determining the age of the petitioner in front of the magistrate and later on the power given in sec 7 of act 2000 were not used properly and the petition was not move forward along with the documents which should be done by the authority with respect to the jurisdiction but case was sent to the trial to the court room the court also did not enquire about the age of the juvenile second the document presented by the petitioner which were licensed for the bail executed with the help of the aid the senior most session judges enquire about the age and found that the the petitioner show cast age less than 18 year age with accordance to the date of 2002 in the month of April and looked as a juvenile so proper enquiry was done by the order of the court and an help in aid form was provided to the juvenile using them principal magistrate in the juvenile Justice Court third under section 6 subclause two of the act 2000 to look out the behaviour the enquiry was set up by the authority with the section 49 of the act 2000 to find the will power of the age of accused search questions or not objected or raised during the trial force The bail was presented in the court and the view was accepted by the sessions court that the bail should be granted to the juvenile and the petition was allowed in this case.

In the case **Mahendra Singh versus State of Rajasthan** the court kept the view that a accused to be confronted where trial under motive planned murder the trial judge awarded him penalty of life imprisonment the accused Appeal to the court that he is less than 18 years of [1]age and he's juvenile as per the juvenile Justice act 2000 and therefore the " This view and accepted him as a JUVENILE and were sentence was not carried forward.

In the case brother Pramod Kumar Shetty versus state of Orissa the court took in decision was made by the court in providing aid to the accused by the order of the High Court first the enquiry was set up in reference to find out the age of the juvenile by the authority through police officer or a magistrate of first class Second this authority should made every enquiry and have power to figure out the detail age through records available or presented by the accused finding the exact date of age of the juvenile third the date of the offence should be formed by this authority to find out the motive behind the act as per mention in the section 2 of the act which defines And the proper date should be found out through this

In the case **Vikrant Kumar Sonu versus state of Uttar Pradesh** grivences complaint filled was launched towards the applicant on the offence and regarding to section 377 511 of IPC when the charge sheet was admitted in the court of law the appelent claim that himself to be a juvenile to as defined in the definition of JUVENILE Justice act and was favour to be accepted by each and every ways in the presence of judge High Court allowed this revision petition and set up at the appellate court order the applicant filed up plaint that you need to be declared juvenile and the complainant differ from the view of appellant take on the view in the trial court choose is that over a period of time no serious actions were taken by court but the records of the national inter-school where he was born the school certificate submitted the report on the age of the juvenile need to kept this view and method of JUVENILE reminding the age the court observed that the it's failure to record any response in the testimony of complainant make it clear and clean that the complainant has been manipulating the appealant and the High Court observe that the document were related to

CHAPTER THREE

CHAPTER 3 CONSTITUTIONAL PROVISION AS PROVIDED

Constitution provision

after the independence in the past 70 years many Constitution articles are present Which provide safety And care education nutrition of children with specific emphasis on protecting fundamental rights and directed states of policy briefly list of articles given below

article 15 sub clause 3 talk about state responsibility for women in general children in making special provision

article 21A talk about right to education it is the duty of the state to provide free and compulsory education to all children in the age group of 6 to 14 years

article 23 talk about traffic in human being and bonded labour it was a bit prohibit any form of bonded forced labour beggar and trafficking of any human being promote in the right of protecting the rights of children's

article 24 talks about working of children in factories hazardous mills Prohibit any children below the age of 14 from working in industries

article 30 E under dpsp provide health and strength of the children should not be abused and

F talk about providing ample labour protect opportunity to children to enjoy their childhood and not get exploited under any condition

DETERMINING AGE OF THE JUVENILE

it is the responsibility power given to the court to decide and make a decision on age of the accused involved in crime act as the child in young age cannot be kept in prison with adult criminal or in jail special power are given in jja act to board authorities in making case and provide punishment on the basis of the documents such as school certificate municipal certificate and certified copy or through medical test it all records are submitted and then age is decided.

In the 1986 at the age of the juvenile is accepted as 16 year for both boys and girls but later on there were some changes in the age by the year 2000 the age was fixed by the government as 18 year for both boys and girls proper definition were given in the recent act 2015 the juvenile was defined

And heinous crime the juvenile to be treated as adult above 16 yr age and age to be decide on the date of crime and record mentioned and accepted in court with scrutiny done with certified copy original through this court decide whether the child is juvenile age or not if not found under age than to be treated as adult and many cases fake certificate are made by school authorities which later on proved wrong and age is not accepted by court proper inspection inquiry are conducted and done regarding scrutinising the age as its lawyers need to prove it verified with original than accepted otherwise medical test various are present with rapid improvement in technology which give results on by conducting test with the help of medical doctors experts

Jja 2015 has solved much extend this problem and with other provision also provide support and safety to children teenage as by through Indian penal code crpc criminal procedure code and main principle of doliincapax which help chidren of age group of 7 to 11 as they are not mature enough to be giving consideration and consent.

The court accepts after scrutiny of documents presented by the school records which were submitted during time of admission with passing the matric exams others documents are also considered as municipal authority which are given on birth death by records and also in some cases the medical examination are done on medical test such as bone test and x-rays and ossification test teeth present.

In the case **Emperor versus Mohammed** here the court ordered that the act committed by that children of throwing stones towards the train their children are being protected under the IPC 80 to 183 of Indian penal code as they wereFive and eight years of age

In case **Ashwini Kumar Saxena versus state of Madhya Pradesh** here the accused was charged with 302 of the IPC with 27 of arms act and with 34 of IPC the offence committed was on the day 19 October 2008 at 12:30 near the area of Chhatarpur which resulted in death of Yadav before the session Court they accused filed a petition in CJM court regarding the age of proving to be a juvenile and bail plea was also presented before the court CJM court CJM court order the bone test and very various other medical test with ex ray result of as a result of rest elbow leg knee and teeth with the opinion of the doctor it was clear that he was 20 years of age from the date of committing offence and the teeth x-ray teeth teeth came to be 32 teeth which resulted in making age more than 21 years has The court order that he's not juvenile at the time of offence.

In the case **Om Prakash versus State of Rajasthan** here the accused was tried of the committing offences under 376 of IPC and they have stand and plead guilty in the case one ground was availed whether by learn it counsel which claim that the accused is juvenile as per the definition of the juvenile Justice act 2000 the court trial ordered the juvenile test that at the date of the incident Was he the juvenile and the result came in school mark admission records and other medical test which prove that he was under her age of 18 And was treated for the rest as juvenile.

In the case **Umesh Chandra versus State of Rajasthan** A complete bench of apex court was sitting on the question of date of commission of offence at the fixed date for convening date of child act the view that was accepted as act apply on from the date and crime committed from that date the children juveniel mens rea need to be questioned to find motive crime act and crime reason if need to be treated as adult the question of enforcement of record and rule act passed was also examined and view were accepted as follows the act enforced through out our country.

In the case **Umesh Chandra versus state of Rajasthan** the court forward the petition with problem to the Constitution bench in which date of commission of offence ? date of application of the act 1986 and 2001 WERE question and the court overruled Das judgement and kept its view straightforward as the age of the juvenile totally depend on the date of the offence not on when he was produced in court or produce in the front of the authority only an offence the age matter.

In the case **Jabbar Singh versus Dinesh** and others the court specifically point out the date of beginning of the trial in which the respondent number one submitted the admission form college data school record and there were difference in certificate which pacifically mention the age hence it became no further Acepted as evidence as a rule are laid down as per section 35 of Indian evidence act and by proper authority checking and enquiry done by the order of the court the difference was observed and it did not fulfil the condition of section 35 of Indian evidence act so as per the date of commencement of the offence the age of the respondent one were given a timeframe and by the age completed on the date IN YEAR 2006 The court ordered that that the respondent would no longer be treated as a juvenile and time given to him to fulfil all condition of evidence act and presenting evidence of age of the school certificate was Over and the offence comitted now be treated as adult

In the case **Dharambir versus State of NCT of Delhi** the court ordered that though the

query of the deciding the age of the Juveniel from now onwards not on the plan on the field and who has admitted no no longer can claim as per juvenile under 1986 act the offence committed by the juvenile should be treated as they have not completed the age of 18 year and the rules through 2000 act declare the juvenile should be brought forward in the court and the trial should be done on the basis of 2000 jja act.

In the case **Ram Suresh Singh versus Prabhas Singh Chotu Singh and** other the respondent number one change the stance within the due process of trial as per police station case number 102 of two 2003 in committing homicide of Tribhuvan Singh the principal magistrate of juvenile Justice board of the state ordered in 2005 August that the age of the respondent number one differ into 20 year extra as the files and the facts and evidence produced by the respondent number one no longer deter mind to be false fabricated and [1]are in a inadmissible in law the file produced by him follow the due process of law is authentic and scrutinised and it is accepted as exception totally depend on as per the case of Mohan Marley and state of Madhya Pradesh the Supreme Court observed that the date of the case differ from the state of hair where the juvenile Lal changed its stance into minor when the during of the course of the offence and has already completed extra duration in the sentence so as per section 15 of 2000 with the rule 98 of 2007 and 64 of the act the court allowed the attraction of way forward involved in the direct conflict the launch fourth with in the bail is accordingly further appeal to be disposed.

Similarly in the case **Lal Mohammad was the state** the court observed that the faculty document on state of representative leads to the greater loss of the evidentiary value and as per the record of following Indian evidence act the other records or observed and the main focus was done on the medical board which conducted the test of the Petitioner and gave the results so here the medical importance were given more priority then other documents on determining age of the juvenile.

In the case **Rattan Lal versus state of Rajasthan** there was aid provided by the High Court under the supervision of authority first there were no enquiry made by the authority in determining the age of the petitioner in front of the magistrate and later on the power given in sec 7 of act 2000 were not used properly and the petition was not move forward along with the documents which should be done by the authority with respect to the jurisdiction but case was sent to the trial to the court room the court also did not enquire about the age of the juvenile second the document presented by the petitioner which were licensed for the bail executed with the help of the aid the senior most session judges enquire about the age and found that the the petitioner show cast age less than 18 year age with accordance to the date of 2002 in the month of April and looked as a juvenile so proper enquiry was done by the order of the court and an help in aid form was provided to the juvenile using them principal magistrate in the juvenile Justice Court third under section 6 subclause two of the act 2000 to look out the behaviour the enquiry was set up by the authority with the section 49 of the act 2000 to find the will power of the age of accused search questions or not objected or raised during the trial force The bail was presented in the court and the view was accepted by the sessions court that the bail should be granted to the juvenile and the petition was allowed in this case.

In the case **Mahendra Singh versus State of Rajasthan** the court kept the view that a accused to be confronted where trial under motive planned murder the trial judge awarded him penalty of life imprisonment the accused Appeal to the court that he is less than 18 years of [1]age and he's juvenile as per the juvenile Justice act 2000 and therefore the " This view and accepted him as a Juveniel and were sentence was not carried forward.

In the case brother Pramod Kumar Shetty versus state of Orissa the court took in decision was made by the court in providing aid to the accused by the order of the High Court first the enquiry was set up in reference to find out the age of the juvenile by the authority through police officer or a magistrate of first class Second this authority should made every enquiry and have power to figure out the detail age through records available or presented by the accused finding the exact date of age of the juvenile third the date of the offence should be formed by this authority to find out the motive behind the act as per mention in the section 2 of the act which defines And the proper date should be found out through this

query with regarding to the criminal offence taken place and exact age when the offence take place the court also relied on the Arnit Das order.

In the case a **hemal Mein versus the state of Jharkhand** the appellant submitted the plaint before the high court that he's been falsely involved in the case and put up in the charge sheet and court records he claimed he is a juvenile The lower court was ordered by the High Court to consider the appellant request of proving age to be juvenile and depend totally on the evidence produced before the lower court entertaining the age of Juveniel.

In the case of **Motilal versus state ofBihar** the applelant came forward to the High Court against the judgement given by the additional session judge of the region Gowda bihar convicting the appellant and ordering the penalty of rigourous imprisonment for the time period of two years the appelent in the High Court submitted plaint with the copy of attested school certificate which was submit by the appellant while taking admission in the year of 1975 in the month of August and which clearly shows that age of the appellant is not less than 18 year of age High Court High Court kept this view and refused the appeal of the appellant On the ground that he has already completed the age of the juvenile and he is adult on the date of commission of the offence and should be tried as an adult and he has to complete the penalty and punishment given by the lower court.

In the case of **Girish versus state of Kerala** the judgement given by the court resulted in the conviction and sentenced imprisonment imposed on the appellant under the section 394 of IPC revision petition was presented before the court in which the appellant claim to be juvenile on the basis of the document issued by the school head principle which clearly defined his age while he was studying the document produced before the court as an evidence show cast the age that he was born on 3 May 1974 and the crime held the date of offence at the night in May 1989 when he was under the age of 16-year-old and was [1]accordance to this documentary days as a juvenile this clearly presented in the prayer of the plaint so that lawsuit could be quashed by the court the court kept the view of the juvenile Justice act 2000 and held responsibility of the first class magistrate all chief judicial magistrate to exercising their all power and responsibility and duty provided under the JJ act and considering all the possibility of rules under the Kerala act Order of the magistrate by providing power under the 482 of CRPC and the chief judicial magistrate should exercise this power as provided in the juvenile Justice act 2000 so in this case duty of the magistrate were clearly defined and kept in the view while treating the juvenile with care and protection.

In the case **Om Prakash versus State of Uttaranchal** in this case the court observed the viewpoint of the on the juvenile order concerning the age of appellant and a competing with

Each other as raise the question that he's turn Julveniel on the time of the crime No evidence were brought forward which gives rights to the appellant the fact of the case were he has started the financial institution account in the Punjab national bank at Dehradun in the Uttaranchal region with keeping the view of this account High Court and the trial court took the view that he might not need to use this account as he might turned to be adult from being minor and could have open the account in other bank and he has not declared to be himself the Supreme Court in this regard reopen and the method of the trial court and said that he could not be defaulter on the basis of this case.

In the **K Surender Singh with the state of Uttar Pradesh** the apex court found that the that nobody can be accepted or raised via means of the accused that he is juveniel and the court are empowered to find the required method and enquiry in finding the age of the accused in the absence of such requests by juvenile.

In the case **Vikrant Kumar Sonu versus state of Uttar Pradesh** grivences complaint filled was launched towards the applicant on the offence and regarding to section 377 511 of IPC when the charge sheet was admitted in the court of law the appelent claim that himself to be a juvenile to as defined in the definition of juveniel Justice act and was favour to be accepted by each and every ways in the presence of judge High Court allowed this revision petition and set up at the appellate court order the applicant filed up plaint that you need to be declared juvenile and the complainant differ from the view of appellant take on the view in the trial court choose is that over a period of time no serious actions were taken by court but the records of the national inter-school where he was born the school certificate submitted the report on the age of the juvenile need to kept this view and method of Juveniel reminding the age the court observed that the it's failure to record any response in the testimony of complainant make it clear and clean that the complainant has been manipulating the appealant and the High Court observe that the document were related to

high school admission was accepted the plea filed by the complainant were defeated and miserably failed

To convince the court and later on a medical opinion was also obtained on this case which clearly gives the result that the person is Juveniel.

In the case **Vijay Singh versus State of Uttar Pradesh** the court considered the truth and accepted the revision petition filed by the appellate in order of the judgement passed by the additional sessions judge a fast track court was made in Agra rejecting the all the plea taken by the juvenile and later on sending the case to the juvenile judge as they were different means and overburden of the courts "and the fact of the case is well on determining the age of the juvenile that committed on date of the offence and the party surrender to the authority and not flee from the location after the commencement of the crime with inconsistent to the 1986 act the advantages provided under section 20 of 2000 act which maintain the location and reference delay before the making sufficient ground in the trial as the date of enforcement of the new act was pending the lawsuit concluded on the provision of the 1986 act which make it clear How to deal with the juvenile and how to promote care and protection and on determining the age of Juveniel as he was under age of 15-year-old

In the case of master **Rajiv Shankarlal versus office in charge of police Station** Malad and others therefore first information report was launched on the accused under the IPC 302307 the case were given forward to the session Court where the petitioner has claimed to be the age of 22 years and became arrested and the trial was started he was put up in jail as a prisoner session Court find out that the age of the accused could be under the age of 22 years therefore the enquiry was set up by the board in the front of the authority in the juvenile Justice board and instructions were given by the court that the accused should not be shifted from observation home to the other place

The instruction of the session Court with reading of the section 49 of the act 2000 no longer help in finding the age of the accused on the basis of the section later on in this case as the time passes by a PIL was filed by the Bombay High Court on behalf of the accused to claim that the he's been illegally detained in the prison and there is a violation of the juvenile Justice act 2000 and his constitutional rights are being violated with the violation of the fundamental rights the session judge also taken enquiry in this case with the certain powers provided and 49 section of the act 2000 once the accused was shifted from home on the request of the juvenile Justice board the observation home provided every food clothes shelter to the juvenile a 15,000 order was passed to be given to juvenile as a repayment and the Supreme Court latest judgement of Gopinath Ghosh versus state of West Bengal and in Barasat Sheila versus union of India these all judgement were kept in record while deciding the merits of this case in addition in 2003 the hours session Judge and additional sessions judge came aware of this petition and order the Thane jail authority to implement the order of the High Court and observation made by the authority in the observation homeLater on the deciding

the prayer of the plaint the court order the repayment of the Rs.15,000 taken from the petitioner and consider him to be a juvenile.

In the case **Mohammed Arif versus State of Rajasthan** High Court given direction and discovered that the ACJM did not go along with the opinion of the medical board which was based on the result conducted medical test that the accused is up between the age of 16 to 18 years of age The decision was taken on the basis of the voter listing and ENrolling the accused and the builder body which looks inside the court and the court observed that he also did not allow any type of cross examination of the witnesses not have received or find any enquiry regarding the evidence given in the present case with the documentation of the file therefore the High Court set aside the order given by the ACJM and Directed sessions judge to initiate the enquiry within the time frame and confirm the age of the accused of the petitioner with all given possibility of a level and listen to the both side and give rise request of coal cross-examination of also all the wetness within the timeframe for one month from the date of receipt of the present case.

In the case of **Manjujouti versus a state** after the direction of the complainant the fir was launched on the opposite party the father of the juvenile came forward with their documents which said that his son is a juvenile beside the oral evidence they don't have any evidence documentary Which reveals that the accused is Juveniel hence the court ordered the ossification test to confirm the age of the juvenile and which resulted in medical test results came in which confirms that he is not a Juveneil and he has also accepted in the trial in the session court that he is 21 years of age the court realise that the false evidence of age were given by the parent and the accused was no longer treated as a juvenile.

In the case **Lalan Singh was a state of Uttar Pradesh** during the trial in the session Court in the area Chandauli of Uttar Pradesh observed that the new act passed with the assent of the Pre[1]sident on the year 2000 and became publicise in the official gazette it in December 2000 and Hence That was applicable to the whole part of India and hence notification were given by the court to enact the act and decides the cases on the basis of of the Present act of juvenile Justice act 2000 from the month of April 2001.

Delhi nirbhya rape case

Nirbhya and his friend were returning home in delhi from movies where the use bus as mode to travel one of the boy who was minor asked them to enter in the bus with black windows and 6 men raped her one of the six was a minor of 17 yr age on 16 december 2012

Later on nirbhya died due to various injury in the private parts and multiple organ failure on 29 december all accused were after a long legal battel were given death penalty one two died in prison and left out executed in by hanging there was a total anger in public toward increase in women sexual crimes and rape and one of the reason was the minor who was 17 and was given others punishment as he was minor and did not got death penalty as heinous crime age limit laws were not changed government changed law and fixed age 16 yr for heinous crime and to be treated as adult.

Archarna kumari vs state of bihar

Petitioner was married with opposite party on 9/6/2014 she was assaulted and asked 5 lakh she complained to authority and police recorded fir and arrested others in which no 2 accused was a juvenile records were presented in court that school certificate the person is 15 yr old the records were scrutinised and than found provisional and original the mistake done by board was recorded and the high court ordered the immediate release of the juvenile the matter was listed in high court in 2021 and decided in no 2 accused was released on the order of the high court.

In case **anil Chaudhary vs state of bihar**

The applants were put on trial for offences ynder 366 a of the penal code and further charged with 376 of ipc found guilty of both the offences while determining age on the basis of the radiological examination may not be an accurate determination and sufficient margin either way has to be allowed yet the totality of the fact stated above with read with the report of the radiological examination leaves room for ample doubt with regards to the correct age of the prosecutrix the benefit of the aforesaid doubt naturally must go in favour of the accused.

CONCLUSION AND SUJIESTIONS

Conclusion

In determining age of the juvenile the amendments are made on the reducing 18 yr age to 16 yr age so that crime committed heinous crime the juvenile can be treated as an adult as juvenile has complete knowledge of means rea in comiting that offence and consequences of the criminal act this is the welcome step than question arises on the how to check age of the juvenile medical test could be done or school certificate is checked in many cases fake schools certificate are produced and misused to determine age in some cases fake medical test are also done to give different result so the court on the facts of the case can order

inquiry through teams on the both methods and can order test on the basis of the facts of the cases new modern technology and new methods improvement in rules and regulation are required to determine age and on controlling crime rate data and protecting child hood the new methods of care and protection need to be done on the child so that need not to fall under the crime the behaviors and needs of child should be checked upon so that just to look cool in society one does not comit any crime. New amendments and methods need to be adopted with from common legal system country so that better justice system can be availed and justice for all to be fulfilled. the recommendations of the Justice J. S. Verma

Suggestion

Juvenile Justice board

Are uniform education system need to be implemented for the education of the child from 1 to 18 years of age all State showed should accept this policy and if changes need to be made state can make changes according to the required state

Area where the board conduct meeting enquiry should be children friendly wearing of black coats police uniform should be avoided to make it friendly with the juvenile

Necesassary infrastructure need required in the by the authority such as latest technology computers stenographer type writer should be supplied and easy access by the board

document should be preserved and scrutinised in a proper manner

in shelter homes The inspection should be made and wardens are provided with all facility in controlling any fight between the juveniles

parents should be allowed to meet with the juvenile and a doctor should be provided which take care of their health and mental health

How to treat a juvenile

should be came forward within the 24 hours in front of the board should be ask about the date of commencement of the crime motive men's Rea behind the crime.

rights of the juvenile should be explain to the juvenile by the board is constitutional and fundamental rights should be explained by the board or authority or by police

right to bail should be explained

the judges in the board should be explain the consequences and the nature of the trial

the home should be kept in a proper manner so that JUVENILE take shelter in it infrastructure should be improved

parents and guardians should be allowed to meet.

In the process of enquiry

principal magistrate are given power and duty to conduct such enquiry and help the board in conducting enquiry within the limited time frame of 4 to 5 months

proper implementation of the act throughout the whole territory of the India

domestic police need to be

Taken in action in enquiring locally and gathering information locally the member of the board should be friendly nature and showed conduct enquiry without uniform and should not beat or harass Any JUVENILE

parents should be informed by the member of board or by local police

Observation home safe home

separate room should be provided to all juvenile weather recording of the age no longer be treated as a hard-core criminal as treated in jail

9 798886 418408

Printed by Libri Plureos GmbH in Hamburg,
Germany